HOW I KEPT MY SELF-WORTH

Surviving Abuse, Hurt and Pain

Linda Tumelo

www.TrueVinePublishing.org

How I Kept My Self-Worth
Linda Tumelo

Published by
True Vine Publishing Co.
810 Dominican Dr. Ste. 103
Nashville, TN 37228
www.TrueVinePublishing.org

ISBN: 978-1-962783-26-2 Paperback
ISBN: 978-1-962783-27-9 eBook

Printed in the United States—First printing

Table of Contents

How I Kept my Self-worth "
Surviving Abuse, Hurt and Pain

From the words of Dr. Martin Luther King, Jr., "Don't allow anybody to make you feel that you are nobody. Always feel that you count, always feel that you have worth, and always feel that your life has ultimate significance."

Telling my story is not to bring shame or embarrassment to my family; it's for my own healing and to inspire and help others in their healing.

I use scriptures throughout this book because everything you want to know about life is found in God's words. As it is written, "All Scriptures in the Bible are God-breathed and are useful for teaching, rebuking, correcting, and training in righteousness" (2 Timothy 3:16).

CHAPTER 1
Abusive Parents

My mother's father was a minister and a strong disciplinarian, but the beatings he gave his children would be considered abuse today. My mother told us her father beat one of her sisters so badly, she passed out, but her mother was meek and humble. My mother had an abusive father and then married an abusive man (my father). I don't condone a man abusing a woman, but I believe my father justified his abuse of my mother because she used her words as a weapon to hurt him. I don't think my mother ever loved my father. I believe she married my father because she was pregnant.

My mother was never physically abusive to her children, but she also used her words to hurt them. We all have heard the phrase, "Sticks and Stones may break my bones, but words will never hurt me." On the contrary, the damage done by verbal abuse and hurtful words is sometimes impossible to rectify or repair.

"Let no corrupting talk come out of your mouths, but only such as is good for building up, as fits the occasion, that it may give grace to those who hear." (Ephesians 4:29)

My father received a lot of respect and praise from his parents and siblings. I believe he was expecting the same from my mother, but they both had an excessive need for attention and admiration, so I don't believe they accommodated each other.

After over ten years of marriage and my mother giving birth to ten children (seven girls and three boys), my mother left my father, leaving all 10 of us with him. I don't know how my mother found the strength to leave my father, but I do know she would never have been able to leave an abusive marriage and take ten children with her. I don't blame her for leaving us with our dad.

Almost a year later, my mother filed for divorce and received custody of all seven girls, while my father got custody of the three boys. However, after the boys ran away from my father, my mother ended up with all ten children.

I admired my mother's strength and perseverance in being able to work and care for ten children. Reflecting on the years when my mother was married to my father, I recall her spending hours at a Laundromat washing clothes for a family of twelve. She cooked, cleaned, and took care of ten children while my father worked almost 12 hours a day.

When my mother became a single mother with

ten children, she already possessed the capability and know-how to manage such a large family. However, financially, I am uncertain how she managed to support all ten children. Due to the strong Christian foundation instilled by her father, my mother passed on a strong faith in God to her children. I believe that through prayers, God guided us along the way.

Our first home was a two-bedroom shack in a rough neighborhood, and gradually, we moved into a larger apartment before settling into a home in a nice neighborhood. I remember my mother riding the bus to work and back home every day. Fortunately, we had a supermarket right behind our house, allowing my mother to walk there to get groceries for cooking for ten children. Despite our financial challenges, we never perceived ourselves as poor because we had nice clothes to wear and food to eat. My mother even allowed us to have a dog, adding another mouth to feed.

Every Thanksgiving and Christmas, my mother would prepare a full holiday meal for all ten children. Christmas Eve was particularly magical for us, with what seemed like a hundred gifts under the Christmas tree to open. The house was filled with laughter, the aroma of baked cookies, and our favorite Christmas Eve meal, Gumbo. For my mother, living for her children was a heartfelt commitment.

I will be forever grateful for those wonderful childhood memories. However, when it came to providing food, clothes, and shelter for her children, that was my mother's strength, but throughout the years my mother exhibited signs of having narcissistic personality disorder. While she was never formally diagnosed with any type of mental illness, my research into narcissistic personality disorder led me to realize, "Oh my God, that's what's wrong with my mother."

Narcissistic personality disorder is a mental condition characterized by an inflated sense of one's own importance, a constant need for excessive attention and admiration, and a lack of empathy for others. Adding to that, individuals with narcissistic personality disorder may lead an unhappy life full of disappointments, especially if they aren't favored or admired enough, as they believe they deserve. People with this disorder often struggle to tolerate criticism, defeat, and the perception of not being seen as special or beautiful in others' eyes.

In my mother's case, she frequently caused powerful and damaging psychological rifts between her children. Pitting one sibling against the other, she used conspiratorial secrets, often based on lies, to further poison and destroy the relationships among her children. This manipulation led my sisters to be in constant competition with each other. A narcissistic mother sets up her daughters and sons for inevitable danger due to the nature of her disorder. What I don't understand is how my mother was strong enough to provide for ten children but not strong enough to protect them from abuse. It seems like my mother thought abuse was a normal part of life.

Most parents aspire to provide their children with the best possible life. It's a common notion that parents want their children to have a better life than they ever had. However, narcissistic parents, particularly mothers with daughters, often engage in unhealthy competition. They may resent their children's youth, beauty, and success, leading to criticism or attempts to sabotage their children in various ways. Parents with narcissistic personality disorder struggle to offer their children adequate attention and nurturing. Their sense of entitlement often results in mistreatment of their children.

Despite the negative traits associated with narcissistic personality disorder, individuals with this condition often lack self-awareness about their own worth and possess fragile self-esteem deep down. It's essential for more people to recognize the seriousness of narcissistic personality disorder. Unlike some other mental illnesses, narcissistic personality disorder cannot be treated with medications, and there is no cure. However, individuals with narcissistic personality disorder can undergo talk therapy (psychotherapy) to address and modify their behaviors.

Treatment for narcissistic personality disorder can be challenging due to the individuals' grandiosity and defensiveness, making it difficult for them to acknowledge they have a problem. Narcissistic personality disorder has faced controversy, often stigmatized as a personal choice rather than a mental health disorder. Sharing stories about mental struggles, like my mother's, is essential to draw attention to individuals exhibiting traits of narcissistic personality disorder. This awareness aims to encourage those individuals to seek the help they need.

I hope that by sharing my story, others can find reflections of their own experiences. During my parents' marriage, my father was a great provider for the family, but he displayed verbal and physical abuse towards some of his children. My paternal grandfather was a strong disciplinarian, while my father's mother also was meek and humble. My father's favorite children were my youngest brother and my sister, who were 11 months older than me. Unfortunately, I was one of my father's least favorite children. Parental connections with children can be influenced by various factors, such as responding to characteristics in their children that they also see in themselves.

Characteristics we embrace in ourselves are often celebrated when mirrored in our children, while flaws may draw out negative responses, such as anger or avoidance due to discomfort with our own shortcomings.

My sister, my father's favorite, had a very outgoing personality, and my father considered her the most attractive of all his daughters. Growing up being called "main son" may have contributed to my father's inflated ego, leading him to seek constant recognition and praise. My sister and brother fulfilled these needs for him, providing the admiration he desired. On the contrary, my father consistently emphasized how unattractive I was, causing me to become distant from him. Perhaps, my father interpreted this as a lack of the recognition he sought.

I recall bringing home pictures taken on school picture day, and my father, upon seeing them, told me, "You can take those ugly pictures back to the school." This experience was embarrassing, having to return my school pictures because my father deemed me ugly. While being made to feel ugly could have damaged my self-esteem, I was remarkably resilient as a child, always bouncing back when knocked down. Somehow, I always believed my life had value.

When I was about 5 or 6 years old, I was beaten by my father simply for being in the wrong place at the wrong time. Following an altercation with my mother, my father, in a fit of rage, directed his anger towards me. My mother called the police and showed them the scars on my back from the beating I had endured. Unfortunately, the policeman looked the other way and remained silent. In those days, a man's wife and children were often regarded as his property, leaving me with a profound sense of vulnerability. Aware that I had no one to protect me, I learned to stay out of my father's way. While an adult woman may choose to endure abuse, I firmly believe that when her children are being subjected to harm, it becomes the mother's responsibility to ensure the protection of her innocent offspring.

When I was about 10 years old, my mother took the time to comb my sisters' and my hair and dressed us in lovely dresses in preparation for attending my aunt's wedding. However, as I was getting into the car, my father stopped me abruptly and declared, "you are not going," leaving me behind. The reasons behind his decision were unclear to me. I wondered if he was ashamed of me, thought I wasn't pretty enough to be seen by others, or simply didn't like me. The confusion and hurt led me to cry for hours, grappling with the emotional impact of being excluded from a family event.

As a child, it's challenging to comprehend mistreatment from a parent, and moments of exclusion or rejection can be especially confusing. The uncertainty of whether my father's actions were rooted in appearance, personal preference, or other reasons left me questioning my own worth.

Reflecting on my experiences, I couldn't help but wonder how my father would have treated me if I were born with a birth defect or handicap. This contemplation underscored my belief that genuine love should not be based on a child's physical appearance; rather, it should emanate from the heart, embracing the uniqueness of each individual.

When I was abused by my father as a child, my mother was never strong enough to protect me, but she showed compassion for me. The single most common factor for children who develop resilience is having at least one person that cares about them.

However, the most confusing thing is that when I became an adult, my mother showed a dislike for me as well. I believe my mother saw the strength in me that she did not have, and perhaps it threatened her sense of power.

My father continued to show dislike for me by poking fun at me and calling me names, all while my siblings laughed. He also caused rifts between his children by showing favoritism, having more love for some of his children over others. How I survived my childhood and was able to maintain my self-worth, I just don't know.

When our parents divorced, my siblings and I were estranged from my father for years. When he came back into our lives, my younger siblings were so happy, but they could not understand why I was not as happy. It was because I started remembering how badly he treated me. My father has always instilled in us Exodus 20:12, "Honor your father and mother, so that your days may be long in the land that the Lord your God is giving you."

But when my father passed away, the only siblings who had a close relationship with our father were my oldest and youngest sisters. They did not care how much love the other siblings were showing my father as long as no family secrets were exposed.

My youngest sister, who was making all the arrangements for our father's funeral, was ruthless when she used my sister, who was our father's favorite daughter that had nothing to do with him before he died, to bully and exclude the other sisters from being involved with the funeral arrangements. My oldest sister was deeply hurt about being excluded. She tried to fight back, but with her multiple sclerosis, she was unable to do so.

I was okay with being excluded. I did not feel I deserved the honor. On the day my father passed away, when tears began to fill my eyes, I felt so ashamed. I was not crying because our father was no longer with us; I was crying because I was freed from the guilt of not having a relationship with him. I was freed from not giving him the honor he felt he deserved. People may use the scripture Exodus 20:12 to make you feel guilty about not having a relationship with your abusive parents, but the Bible also states, "Fathers, do not provoke your children to anger, but bring them up in the discipline and instruction of the Lord" (Ephesians 6:4). Additionally, "Train up a child in the way he should go, and when he is old he will not depart from it" (Proverbs 22:6).

The word "honor" in these contexts means respect. So, while it is encouraged to respect your parents and provide financial support if they are in need, no one should feel guilty about not wanting to have a relationship with an abusive parent. If you're feeling unloved by your parents, consider reading Psalm 27:10, which says, "When my father and my mother forsake me, Then the LORD will take care of me."

CHAPTER 2
Sibling Abuse

Throughout my childhood, I was physically tortured by my oldest brother, who was four years older than me. He consistently punched and hit me, and when I was about ten years old, he threw a rock or a piece of glass that hit me in the forehead, requiring stitches and leaving a permanent scar. When I was around 12 years old, during the time when my mother left my father, my brother's torment escalated as my father worked long hours, leaving no other parent in the house.

I remember a particularly intense incident when my brother punched me in the chest so hard that I thought I was going to pass out. The pain felt as if a bone in my chest was broken. Despite crying out to my father for help, he remained asleep in bed after his exhausting workday, showing no concern for my distress. I had no one to confide in about the pain I was enduring. That forceful punch to my chest could have broken my breastbone. As a result, my breastbone is now protruding from my chest. I never sought medical attention to determine whether this protrusion is a birth deformity or a result of a broken breastbone that didn't heal properly when my brother assaulted me.

I don't know how I survived my brother's prolonged abuse that continued for years. It's alarming to realize that children are not safe in their own homes when no adult cares enough to protect them, and sometimes abuse is even encouraged. I recall an incident when my oldest brother, around 15 or 16 years old, began beating my oldest sister, who was just a year older than him, in the bathroom. Upon hearing her screams, my siblings, my mom, and I rushed to see what was happening. I expected my mom to intervene and stop the beating, but to my astonishment, when I looked at her, she had a smile on her face. I couldn't comprehend why my mother would seem pleased that my brother was assaulting my sister. Her failure to intervene in that moment, I believe, opened the door for my oldest brother to abuse his younger siblings.

My parents were divorced when we were all living with my mother, and it was during this time that my oldest brother started abusing my younger siblings. The lack of protection and intervention allowed the cycle of abuse to persist, leaving lasting emotional and physical scars on us. My mother knew my oldest brother was abusing my siblings but did nothing to stop him, even when he tried to murder my younger brother (who was about 10 years old) by tying him to a large ceiling fan in the attic.

We lived in a house with no central air, so the living room ceiling had an opening where the fan from the attic could keep us cool. The first thing we would do when we got home was turn on the ceiling fan, but one day when we came home, before turning on the fan , we heard my brother in the attic screaming for help. We went to the attic to see a disturbing scene. My brother was tied up with his body next to the large blades of the fan. If we would have turned on the fan, it would have cut my brother to pieces. It was obvious that my oldest brother was disturbed, but my mother never tried to remove my oldest brother from the home to protect her other children.

That same brother who was tied to the fan grew up to be over 6 feet tall. He became the protector of the family, and that's when my oldest brother stopped abusing us. My brother's need to be a protector eventually cost him his life at the age of 21 years old when he was shot and killed trying to protect a girl he met from being abused. I've always been a strong person, but it took me years to heal from my brother's death. We all go through stages of grief when we lose a loved one, but you have to find your own way of healing. As evil and disturbed as I once perceived my oldest brother, I came to see him as a scared little boy who was mistreated and unloved. My father's mean, harsh, and physically and verbally abusive behavior towards my oldest brother instilled a deep-seated fear in him. I witnessed the stark contrast as my father showed love to my younger brother while neglecting a loving relationship with my oldest brother.

Research indicates that abused children, who may lack the strength and resilience of others, can undergo permanent changes in the developing brain, leading to psychological and emotional problems. Adults who experienced childhood abuse often turn to drugs and alcohol as a means of self-medicated coping. Unfortunately, my brother battled alcoholism throughout most of his life, highlighting the long-lasting impact of the abuse he endured. When my oldest brother became an adult, he took the courageous step of confronting my dad about the mistreatment he endured as a child and how it negatively impacted his life.

It became evident that hurt people often end up hurting others due to their own pain, fear, sadness, and trauma. The act of causing harm to others may temporarily provide a sense of control and power, but this relief is short-lived. Consequently, the perpetrator remains on a constant search for ways to inflict more pain. It's crucial to recognize that finding solace and feeling good about oneself doesn't have to come at the expense of hurting others.

The choice lies between bitterness and personal growth. One can either allow the challenges they've faced to embitter them or use those experiences to become a better person. It's a choice between allowing adversity to define one's character negatively or using it as a catalyst for positive change and personal development.

I feel incredibly blessed that I chose the path of becoming a better person rather than letting my childhood abuse make me bitter. Instead, I've cultivated compassion for anyone experiencing or who has experienced abuse because I intimately understand the impact it can have on one's emotions and life. Choosing bitterness can come at a significant cost, blocking blessings, prolonging mental and emotional pain, and potentially worsening it. It can also prevent the experience of the potential joys of living a happy life. On the other hand, building others up and extending compassion can lead to a sense of empowerment and fulfillment.

CHAPTER 3

Mental Illness

People with mental illness have often been stigmatized, leading to their fear and shame in discussing mental illness openly. Individuals dealing with a mental disorder should never face blame or shame; instead, they deserve compassion and understanding. Families must not ignore warning signs due to concerns about societal stigma. Prioritizing one's image over seeking help for loved ones is, in my opinion, a selfish approach.

People generally recognize abnormal behavior, yet they tend to overlook warning signs of mental illnesses such as anxiety disorders, depression, bipolar disorder, schizophrenia, or other mental health issues. We often overlook mental illness in mothers. It's challenging for most people to accept the idea that a mother may be incapable of loving and nurturing her own children. I believe that, too often, we place mothers on a pedestal. Placing individuals on a pedestal assumes they are godlike, devoid of human flaws. This approach is only effective for a short time because everyone has flaws; everyone is human. The inevitable result is disappointment when someone fails to live up to unrealistic expectations.

Mothers bear the responsibility of giving birth, caring for their families, and providing financial support, all while potentially dealing with postpartum depression, mental illness, or low self-esteem. Women who have experienced childhood abuse or other traumas face a higher risk of developing mental health conditions. I believe my mother suffered from postpartum depression when she had twins over 60 years ago. She struggled to connect with her twins and was unable to care for them. During that time, diagnoses and treatments for postpartum depression were unavailable, depriving my mother of the help she needed.

For some women, postpartum depression can persist for years. When my mother gave birth to twins, she already had seven other children, all under the age of 10, and a year later, she had another child. With a new baby every year, I believe the continuous physical and mental strain took a toll on her. Despite her desire to control family planning using birth control pills, my father discovered them and discarded them, leaving my mother with no control over her own body. She endured pregnancies every year, while my father led a double life, deceiving her for years.

Being a mother is one of the hardest jobs in the

world, and no one is perfect at it. My mother faced depression and endured verbal and physical abuse, yet she exhibited endless patience, perseverance, resilience, and tolerance while caring for ten children through both good and bad times.

Teenage mothers find themselves in the challenging position of caring for a child when they may not even be able to care for themselves. The stress of lacking resources and support can lead to significant levels of depression.

I have grappled with depression throughout my life and experienced anxiety as an adult due to a desire for more from life. I believed I deserved better than what I had. While prescription medications can be life-saving for many dealing with mental illness, taking antidepressants was not an option for me due to the way they made me feel. Instead, I had to put in the work by changing my thoughts, practicing prayer, exercising, eating healthy, and finding ways to bring comfort to others.

The Bible tells us who "...comforts us in all our affliction, so that we may be able to comfort those who are in any affliction, with the comfort with which we ourselves are comforted by God" (2 Corinthians 1:4).

Mental illness is never your fault, but I believe

that anytime your mood starts affecting your thinking, behavior, and your ability to care for your children, seeking professional help is crucial. Mental illness can leave children emotionally scarred and strain marriages and relationships with friends, but with early intervention, one can lead a positive and fulfilling life.

CHAPTER 4

Statutory Rape

When I was 15 years old, a man who was between 18 to 19 years old started talking to me at my high school. I thought he was a student at my school, but he had already graduated. When he started showing interest in me, I thought I had a boyfriend. I was an unloved child that no one had ever shown attention to, and I never felt attractive, so finally I felt special. He would take me to his house where he lived with his mother to sexually take at advantage of me. I found myself in a situation I was not mature enough to handle and there was no one to protect me.

I was the same age as my granddaughter is now. Observing her innocence, I understand why, in the state of Texas, the age of consent is 17. This means that if an adult engages in any form of sexual activity with a child under 17, it is considered statutory rape – even if the younger individual agreed to the sexual activity.

I would give up my life to protect my granddaughter's innocence and shield her from sexually transmitted diseases, and a pregnancy her body and mind is not ready for. Statutory rape laws are not being enforced enough to protect girls and boys from being taken advantage of. It is estimated that there are more than 7 million incidents of statutory rape every year. However, it is clear that most incidents are not prosecuted and do not lead to convictions. Most men that have sex with children are irresponsible. They don't care about ruing a child's life. They prey on young girls and boys that are not mature enough and don't have life experiences to make decisions that will affect their lives. Research shows that the part of a person's brain that manages judgment is not fully developed until they reach their twenties.

Parents have to protect their children from men and women that prey on children. Children need to be taught to say something if they are being abused, and if it's the parents or any other family member that's abusing a child, we all are obligated to report it.

The man that took advantage of me never took me out on a date like a boy would do with his girlfriend. I quickly realized the man was not a student and he was just taking advantage of me. I wished I was taught the body is not meant for sexual immorality. "Or do you not know that your body is a temple of the Holy Spirit within you, whom you have from God? You are not your own, for you were bought with a price. So glorify God in your body". (1 Corinthians 6:19-20)

While on summer break from school he was not able to pick me up from school to take me to his house and take advantage of me, so I was able to hide out from him. I felt free and I was able to take control of my body, and it made me feel powerful.

I got my first summer job through a summer program for kids ages 14 to 17. When I got my first paycheck, I was so excited to have my own money. I went to the store and brought a perm for my hair. I didn't know what I was doing, so my hair start coming out in my hands. I cried for days. I quit my summer job and hid out in the house for months. My mother made an appointment for me with a beautician to try and correct the damage to my hair.

While at the beauty shop, the man who had been taking advantage of me walked in. It was like all the strength was sucked out of my body because I knew all he wanted was sex. I started slumping in the chair while the hairstylist was finishing up my hair. Sensing my discomfort, she asked, "Do you know that man?" She seemed protective. Before I could respond, he claimed, "Her mama told me to come get her."

I wondered, "Why would my mother tell this man, whom she'd never met, where to find me? Especially when she knew I was avoiding him by not accepting his calls. When he first started calling for me, my mother should have asked, 'Who are you, and what do you want with my daughter?'"

Around the same time my hair fell out, my sister struggled with severe acne that hurt her self-esteem. Whenever someone visited our house, she'd hide under the covers. Instead of taking her to a dermatologist, my mother embarrassed her by showing her acne to our cousin. It puzzled me why my mother cared enough about my hair to send me to a salon.. When my hair fell out that was the first and only time my mother sent me to a hair salon and weeks later after that hair appointment she looked at my hair with disgust and said to me, "You're almost bold headed".

As strange as it may sound, I think my mother intentionally got me out of the house to meet that man. I believe she knew what he wanted from me. It's not normal for a mother to disclose the whereabouts of her underage child to a man.

Maybe my mother felt the need to please others. People-pleasing often comes from tying one's self-worth to what they do for others. Helping others can make people pleasers feel important. However, when you prioritize others' needs over your own children, I believe that's a sickness.

I didn't have the strength to say no and express, "I don't want to go with you," so I ended up leaving with him. As we left the hair salon, he glanced at my hair and asked, "What happened to your hair?" I felt so embarrassed. The beautician had to cut most of my hair off because it was severely damaged. The disapproving look he gave me made me feel incredibly unattractive. It seemed like he didn't care about my appearance; all he wanted was sex, so again he took me to his house to use me for sex. I keep asking myself, "Why did I go with him?" I was old enough to protect myself and say no. Now I realize why I couldn't say no. When my hair fell out, I was devastated and experienced a moment of low self-esteem. The way your hair looks might seem superficial, but for teenage girls, it's normal for their self-esteem to be connected to their appearance and how others perceive them.

When you have low self-esteem, it impacts your self-confidence, and your inner voice may constantly tell you that you are not good enough or worthy. This makes it challenging to stand up for yourself, leading to vulnerability and the likelihood of being taken advantage of. I had to learn to stop blaming myself for not being able to prevent being taken advantage of. Despite my young age, I had the mindset to recognize that I was being taken advantage of and did my best to protect myself.

After he finished having sex with me, he dropped me off at home. I felt so ashamed, dirty and powerless. My mother met me at the front door, never inquiring about the man who brought me home. I felt confused because the woman at the door looked like my mother, yet it felt as if I were facing a stranger. I was so angry that I couldn't bring myself to look at her.

Having always had a strong sense about things, I sensed that my mother's intentions were to embarrass me, much like she did to my sister. She knew I had hidden in the house for months, embarrassed about my hair. What I know now that I didn't understand as a child, my mother was incapable of protecting me or any of my siblings.

As a grown woman with low self-esteem, my mother lacked the strength to shield herself from abuse. Her struggle to value herself made it challenging to protect her children's welfare. While I experienced a moment of low self-esteem, my mother endured years of it, being told and made to feel unworthy and powerless. I've learned that low self-esteem can make one vulnerable to depression. I vividly recall my mother's everyday appearance: a housecoat, no makeup, and uncombed hair.

Low self-esteem permeates almost every aspect of our lives, shaping how we perceive ourselves and react to life's challenges. Yet, it's possible to reclaim your worth by changing your self-perception. Reclaiming your worth and learning to love yourself involves a process known as self-care. It's about nurturing the wonderful person that you are.

Feelings of worthiness can fluctuate for everyone; it's a normal part of life. Acknowledging your own worth helps you recognize that you are a unique, special, and valuable person with control over your life. Rooting yourself in the confidence that God deems you worthy is crucial. As King David expressed in Psalm 139:14, "I will praise You, for I am fearfully and wonderfully made. God doesn't make junk!"

My mother didn't protect me, so I understood I had to fight to protect myself. A week later the man that took advantage of me called for weeks looking for me again for sex. Perhaps, because my own mother had disclosed my whereabouts and my self-esteem was low, he believed he could continue exploiting me. The experience made me stronger, so when he persistently called for weeks, I never accepted his calls. One day, lacking caller ID, I answered the phone unaware it was him. He likely thought, "I finally got her," but to his surprise, I had regained my self-esteem. I firmly said no, accompanied by a few choice words, and he realized it was over. He never called again.

Sometimes, I wonder if my strength to protect myself hadn't prevailed, might I have been vulnerable to further exploitation or even been impregnated again and again. What happened to me left lasting scars, shaping my life in profound ways. I vowed I'd rather face death than allow anyone to make me feel that powerless again.

Throughout my life it has been challenging trying to replace those feelings with a sense of strength and empowerment. I'm suspicious of everyone I meet spotting things about people nobody else even considers are there. When not in control of a situation, anxiety takes hold. I've come to understand that while building walls can serve as a defense mechanism, it creates complications in relationships. It's a constant journey to find balance between self-protection and fostering genuine connections.

CHAPTER 5
Pregnancy

I repressed the memories of what happened to me and continued with my life. However, months later, I discovered I was pregnant. I had just turned 16 so I was terrified of what my mother would say, so I hid my pregnancy for months.

Weighing only 110 pounds, I could no longer conceal my pregnancy. At six months pregnant, my sister informed my mother, but to my surprise, she wasn't upset. Her first words were, "I knew she was pregnant." At that time, I didn't consider that my mother's lack of upset might be tied to her failure to protect me. When my mother took me to the doctor, I don't remember being asked about the male who impregnated me. It still surprises me that when underage girls become pregnant Children Protective Services is not notified? It's sexual abuse of a child. It's different with physical abuse. If a child is showing signs of physical abuse Child Protective Services will be notified and an investigation will begin.

We live in a society that expects women to be more responsible for things that men are not. More blame and responsibility is put on the pregnant teenage girls, but men aged 18 and older produced half of the unwanted teenage pregnancies of girls between 14 and 17.

I left school and stayed home until I had my daughter. When she was around 6 months old, my mom contacted her dad to let him know about his baby girl. When he visited, he offered $20 for child support. My mom declined, saying, "Keep your money, you can't afford it." Instead of being upset with the man who impregnated her underage daughter, she should have insisted on child support.

My mom already had ten children, and I knew she wasn't thrilled about taking on the responsibility of another mouth to feed. I wondered why she wasn't angry – perhaps she was trying to hide her own wrongdoing? She told a man looking for sex where to find her underage daughter. There should have been arrests and convictions for statutory rape and aiding and abetting. My mother never took responsibility for role in helping the man who impregnated me and the man that impregnated me never paid a penny in child support or was made to take responsibly for fathering a child with an underage girl. I was too young to know that in the state of Texas, when an unwed mother receives certain types of public assistance, a child support case may be opened automatically.

The Attorney General's Office ensures that parents fulfill their support obligations as per court orders. I think my mom was aware that if she assisted me in obtaining public assistance, authorities would pursue the father for support. Unfortunately, she made no effort to help me access any public assistance for myself and my daughter. As a result, both my daughter and I were denied the support we deserved.

It was incredibly embarrassing when my daughter's father had the audacity to ask if he could take her to the park. When I insisted he pay child support before taking her anywhere, he argued that he didn't have to because his mother provided support. At the age of sixteen, I found myself being the only one trying to make him take responsibility for fathering a child.

While his mother did supply my daughter with clothes, shoes, and gifts for birthdays and Christmas, it didn't address the pressing need for child support. I needed financial assistance to buy essentials like diapers and food for his child. Child support was crucial for covering rent and ensuring a safe place to live for both me and our daughter. I was simply asking for him to contribute financially to meet the daily necessities of our lives.

My daughter's father never made an effort to support our child or build a relationship with her. When I moved out of my mother's house, the only apartment I could afford was in a low-income area infested with rats and roaches. I had a sofa and a bed, and no car to get around. Despite being an unwed teenage mother with minimal financial assistance, my mother consistently reminded me of my responsibility to my daughter.

I took on jobs that paid barely above minimum wage, given my lack of education. Despite the financial challenges, I managed to secure health and life insurance for both myself and my daughter.

Later on, my sister, too, became an unwed mother around the age of 18 and moved into the same apartment complex where I was living. It felt like we were facing the difficulties together. However, when my sister met a man and got married, she seemed to distance herself from our shared struggles. This hurt me deeply, especially since we had been close growing up. We were inseparable. It was disheartening that, once she married and left behind the rat and roach-infested apartment, she never checked in to see if I was doing okay.

I wondered if my sister was ashamed of me or if she felt she was better off because she was now married and no longer living in challenging conditions. Perhaps seeing me was a reminder of the life she used to have. To this day, my sister has never attempted to rekindle a sisterly relationship with me, leaving me questioning the reasons behind the distance.

The future seemed uncertain for me. Although I obtained my GED, I was unsure about my life's direction and what I wanted to become. Most of my days were filled with struggles, yet a voice inside me reminded me of my self-worth. Despite facing numerous challenges, I never gave up hope that one day my life would take a positive turn.

CHAPTER 6
My Mother's Hate

My mother's hate for me grew worse over the years. One summer, my uncle kindly sent me an airline ticket to visit California. My daughter was happily spending her vacation with her aunt, so it seemed like the perfect time for me to take a break. While staying with my uncle and enjoying a much-needed vacation, my mother called and accused me of neglecting my responsibilities to my daughter. The conversation took a dark turn as she started yelling and using hurtful words calling me a bitch and a whore. The intensity of her anger and hatred left me in shock, as this was the first time she had ever spoken to me in such a way.

I couldn't comprehend her behavior. Was she perhaps envious that I was enjoying a vacation she wished she could have taken? The impact of this upsetting experience was so profound that I felt like I had an out-of-body experience. I sensed psychological shock, feeling emotionally numb and detached from my body, and my mind became foggy. Although I can't recall exactly what I said in response to my mother, I do remember hanging up on her.

Reflecting on the situation, I recalled how my

mother had told the man who fathered my child that he couldn't provide financial support. Yet, she cursed me when she believed I was neglecting my daughter. The inconsistency in her actions left me bewildered and hurt. Just like all the other times my mother showed narcissistic behavior and hate for me, I just swept it under the rug and forgot about it.

My daughter fell ill during her last year of college and had to leave her car and personal belongings with our cousin while she recovered. Unfortunately, our cousin allowed her boyfriend to use my daughter's car without her permission. Determined to retrieve my daughter's belongings, I devised a plan that, with God's help, proved successful. However, to my surprise, our cousin was upset that I intervened to help my daughter. She reached out to my mother, and I'm unsure how she knew my mother would turn against me.

My mother, without consideration for my safety, disclosed my whereabouts to our cousin, who threatened to harm me. It's disheartening to see a mother's actions potentially endangering her own child. While the Bible emphasizes the importance of a mother's love in 1 Kings 3:16-28. In this chapter, we find the story of two ladies going to King Solomon with a problem. One woman said,

"Your Majesty, we both live in the same house. Recently, my baby was born at home, and three days later, her baby was born. It was just us two there. One night, while we were all asleep, she accidentally rolled over on her baby, and he died. Then, without me knowing, she took my son from my bed, placed him in her bed, and put her dead baby next to me. When I woke up in the morning to feed my son, I realized he was dead. But when I saw him in the light, I knew he wasn't my child."

"No way!" the other woman exclaimed. "He was your son. My baby is alive!"

"The dead baby is yours!" argued the first woman. "Mine is alive!"

They kept on arguing until King Solomon intervened. He said, "Both of you claim this live baby is yours. Bring me a sword."

A sword was brought, and Solomon commanded, "Cut the baby in half! This way, each of you can have a part of him."

The real mother pleaded, "Please don't harm my son, Your Majesty! I love him dearly. Give him to her, just don't hurt him!"

The other woman callously said, "Fine, cut him in half, so neither of us gets the baby."

Solomon, with wisdom, said, "Do not harm the

baby." He pointed to the first woman, declaring, "She is his real mother. Give the baby to her."

People in Israel were amazed by Solomon's decision. They realized that God had granted him wisdom to understand the strength of a mother's love.

A mother's love is powerful, as seen in God's words.

However, God knows that not all mothers love their children, as written in Isaiah 49:15-18, "Can a mother forget the baby at her breast and have no compassion on the child she has borne? Though she may forget, I will not forget you!" This verse reminds us that even when we don't have the love of our earthly mothers, there is a higher love and care that transcends human shortcomings.

We should hold parents responsible for the harm they caused their children, but parents who abuse their children get a slap on the wrist and probation, take a few parenting classes, and then they are fit to be a parent again until their children end up dead.

In our society, we believe that parents have rights and children belong with their parents, especially moms, which makes children more vulnerable to physical, emotional, and psychological abuse , but children have the right to be protected and the right to live.

CHAPTER 7
Finding my Purpose

My life changed significantly when I was baptized at the age of 17. It truly felt like a rebirth for me. Putting on Christ through baptism was a meaningful experience, especially since I was part of a congregation where I received more love than I had from my own family.

The congregation was led by admirable men who exemplified love and kindness, and they encouraged all members to do the same. It was within this community that I met my first real boyfriend, and I was treated with respect despite being an unwed mother. We enjoyed typical boyfriend-girlfriend activities, going on dates and spending time together.

However, when he introduced me to his family during Thanksgiving, they disapproved of our relationship. I understood their concerns, as he was only 18 with his whole life ahead of him, and being with an unwed teenage mother might not have seemed ideal. Consequently, he decided to end our relationship. Despite the heartbreak of being dumped by my first boyfriend, I never felt devalued.

After landing a job that paid more than minimum wage, I faced the disappointment of being laid off after two years, which left me feeling at an all-time low. Plunging into a deep depression, I then learned about an opportunity to volunteer for my church's senior citizens program. That decision turned out to be transformative.

Years prior, I had prayed for guidance from God to reveal my talents, realizing that sitting at an office desk doing paperwork didn't bring me happiness. God had already bestowed talents upon me, but I had remained within my comfort zone, hopping from one job to another without finding contentment. It took a job loss for me to recognize that God was urging me to step out of my comfort zone and utilize the talents He had given me.

Even without a college degree, I discovered that my creative talents were valuable. The turning point came when I started volunteering with the Church's senior citizen program, where I found a fulfilling outlet for my creativity. As the Bible reminds us in (1 Peter 4:10) "Each of you should use whatever gift you have received to serve others".

After volunteering for four months with the senior citizen program, the director recognized my dedication and offered me a permanent position. I embraced the opportunity to work using the talents that

God had blessed me with. In my role, I provided vital information on nutrition, organized memory-improvement games, taught arts and crafts classes, conducted healthy eating sessions, led line dancing, and coordinated birthday parties. I felt a deep sense of purpose, knowing that I was enhancing the quality of life for the senior citizens I served.

Interestingly, my mother was also part of the senior citizen program. Most seniors appreciated my hard work, and some even thanked my mother for giving birth to me. However, there was one individual in the program who harbored animosity towards me. This person went to the program director, spreading lies and prompting an investigation into false accusations against me.

I was baffled by this hostility until one day when the senior approached me and accused me of having no respect for my mother. This took me by surprise because I had never shown any disrespect to my mother, whether at the senior program or in other aspects of my life. The false accusations left me facing unwarranted scrutiny, but I remained committed to my work and the positive impact it had on the seniors.

After finishing work that evening, I called my mother to inquire about the accusations made by the senior citizen at my job, claiming I disrespected her. To my surprise, my mother remained silent. Pressing further, I asked if she had been talking about me, yet again, she said nothing.

The next day when my mother came to the senior program, she looked at me, rolled her eyes, then went over to the senior citizen that said to me, "you have no respect for your mother", kissed her on the cheek. I knew something was not right with my mother's behavior; I just had a difficult time putting my finger on what was wrong. Her conduct exhibited signs of someone with narcissistic personality disorder, a term I was unfamiliar with back then.

In typical situations, mothers take pride in their children's achievements and want them to succeed. However, instead of supporting me, my mother attempted to undermine my relationships with the senior citizens I worked with. Struggling to comprehend her behavior, I chose to bury the incident, avoiding any further discussion about it. Facing adversity, I was determined not to let anyone undermine the senior citizen program I had worked hard to build. After it was proven that the senior citizen who accused me had lied, she left the program.

When the senior citizen program ended, my niece informed me of a position as an activity coordinator at the property where she worked as the Property Manager. Despite being hired immediately due to my skills and experiences, my niece later attempted multiple times to get me fired. Confused and concerned, I turned to my family for answers, only to be met with hostility and anger from my sister (my niece's mother) and, surprisingly, my own mother, who seemed to lead the opposition.

Even reaching out to my youngest sister's husband who is an Elder of Church in a position where it was his responsibly to intervene. The Bible tells us in, (1Timothy 3:4-5) "If an Elder does not know how to manage his own family, how can he take care of God's church?" Despite his role, he did nothing to stop my youngest sister from trying to discredit me. She continued her efforts by telling my niece things I had allegedly said about her and accusing me of attempting to take her job. It was very puzzling, as I was hired as an activity coordinator and genuinely enjoyed using the talents God had given me. At times, my confidence might be perceived as over-confidence, leading people to see me as controlling, arrogant, or competitive—traits that don't align with my true character.

A meeting was arranged with my supervisor, niece, and myself to address the issue of my niece's persistent attempts to get me fired. Surprisingly, during the meeting, there was no discussion about my job performance. Instead, my niece looked at me with a sense of hatred and uttered, "My family told me to watch my back with you." Hearing those words inflicted deep emotional pain, and I couldn't help but think, "I'm your family, too." It became clear that my family played a significant role in shaping my niece's negative attitude towards me.

My supervisor understood that my niece's motives were personal, and I began to realize that my family dynamics were influencing her behavior. Despite having six sisters, I had never experienced conflicts with them. I had always been supportive, babysitting their kids whenever needed and opening my home to help them even when my own resources were limited.

The lack of love and respect from my sister left me bewildered. Reflecting on my family's history of betrayals, backstabbing, and unhealthy competition among sisters, I began to see a pattern. One sister had even attempted to destroy another sister's marriage through a deceitful scheme. Considering the harm my sisters had inflicted upon each other, it became apparent that I, too, could become a target of their destructive tendencies.

When my mom and sisters demonstrated how little love and respect they had for me, my niece started treating me harshly and aggressively. I recalled how my sister, who is also my niece's mother, used severe verbal and physical discipline on her. Research indicates that children exposed to harsh discipline from their parents may grow up to be harsh and aggressive themselves. I believe my sister's strict approach to disciplining her children might have originated from our father.

Feeling angry and filled with rage, I came across a scripture that said, "Humble yourselves, therefore, under the mighty hand of God so that at the proper time he may exalt you" (1 Peter 5:6).

Shortly after starting my job, my niece suffered an ankle injury and was on sick leave for months. I thought maybe that was God's way of giving me an opportunity to prove myself, but once she returned to work, she resumed trying to show that I wasn't doing a good job. During her absence, I made a positive impact on the community, revealing that her attempts to get me fired were personal.

My niece provide me with petty cash each month for community activities, but for nearly a year, she stopped giving me the funds. Perhaps she believed that withholding the petty cash would cause me to fail at my job, or maybe she was pocketing the money. Despite this, my job performance and the residents' needs were never compromised. I utilized my creativity and skills to organize holiday craft sales to fund craft classes, birthdays, and holiday parties.

When my supervisor accused me of requesting too much petty cash, I had to defend myself by explaining that I hadn't received any petty cash from the manager (my niece) for months. The issue of what happened to the petty cash was never addressed again. Despite being resilient since childhood, working with my niece became a source of mental and physical stress. After two years, I decided to resign. Unfortunately, this led to the loss of my job and my home, resulting in me becoming homeless. My mother had moved out of her home, the place where my siblings and I grew up, to live in a retirement community. I believed that her house should have been a refuge for family members facing difficult times.

Regrettably, my mother allowed my sisters to decide to move our brother and his girlfriend into her home. This brother had a history of alcoholism and had physically and sexually abused his siblings, causing turmoil in the family for years within the very same house. I knew my sisters would have never allowed me to move into our mother's house so I can get back on my feet, but why not help my sister with multiple sclerosis?

Her condition confined her to a wheelchair, and the small house she lived in made it challenging for her to move around. I visited her frequently, and if my other sisters had done the same, they would have realized the urgent need for a larger home to improve her quality of life. Our mother's house could have provided the space she desperately needed.

Unfortunately, there was a constant comparison among us about who was doing better and who was not. As I mentioned earlier, my mother had a tendency to pit us against each other, fostering a competitive atmosphere among my sisters. This constant competition made it difficult to genuinely support and uplift each other. It's challenging to build up someone when you're constantly competing with them, as the underlying goal is often to be more successful than the other person.

It's true that some individuals tie their egos to success, leading their pride and self-worth to be determined by their achievements. This can result in toxic competitiveness. The Bible reminds us in 1 John 3:17, "If anyone has material possessions and sees a brother or sister in need but has no pity on them, how can the love of God be in that person?" Facing homelessness, I was fortunate that a cousin I had grow close to offered me a place to live in her home.

CHAPTER 8
Repressed Memories

Facing joblessness and homelessness, I managed to stay resilient. However, when my daughter's father passed away, repressed memories from my childhood resurfaced, hitting me like a ton of bricks. The more than 40 years of my mother's lack of love for me, which hadn't made me feel devalued until then, suddenly weighed heavily on me. The voice in my head that always assured me of my life's value began to fade.

Repressed memories that have been repressed for years have been repressed for a reason; that reason being that when a person goes through significant trauma, the brain shuts down, dissociation takes over and as a survival technique, the trauma(s) get unconsciously blocked and tucked away. When it comes to childhood trauma, your brain may repress memories as a coping mechanism. Throughout adulthood, you might feel something is not right and not know why. Signs and symptoms that indicate you may have repressed memories from childhood trauma. The impact of recovering memories that have been repressed for years can be a debilitating process in your trauma healing. I now understand why I never married; I sabotaged every relationship I had, putting up a shield so I won't be hurt.

I wrote my mother a letter letting her know I remembered what she did to me, when I'd just turned 16 years old. I never shared the letter with anyone else, but my mother made herself the victim. My mother telling a man looking for sex where to find me which resulted in me getting pregnant was too threatening to her sense of self, so she end up denying fault and refusing ownership of her mistake, thereby protecting her self-image.

My family rejected me because they believed I was blaming my mother for not safeguarding me, thinking I should take full responsibility for becoming pregnant at 16. Coming from a highly dysfunctional family, many of my siblings had to confront either our father or mother about their childhood abuse. I asked my oldest sister why I was being punished for addressing my mother's failure to protect me when I was a child.

My mom convinced most of my siblings to turn against me using lies, except for my oldest sister. I don't think my mom shared the details of the letter I wrote to her, but instead, she told them false things to make herself look like the victim. This led my siblings to treat me with a lot of hate. Even when I told them the truth, they still took my mom's side.

Sometimes, siblings who are toxic themselves support a parent who's also toxic. When family members side with the person causing harm, it's often because they don't want to believe the abuse is true. They worry about the family's reputation, the abuser being the head of the household, the fear of exposing family secrets, and other survivors in the family not being ready to talk about their own abuse.

When a family member decides to speak up about their abuse, it's common for other family members to resort to bullying tactics like aggression, manipulation, humiliation, and intimidation. This may include constant criticism, blaming the person regularly, name-calling, and a lack of appreciation or value for the individual.

Family bullies might also resort to gaslighting or turning other family members against the person, including spouses, uncles, aunts, cousins, and even children and grandchildren. In my case, even those not blood-related to my mother portrayed her as the victim.

My oldest sister confronted my mother, suggesting that instead of discussing me with the other siblings, she should talk to me directly. However, my mother dismissed her, claiming I was bringing up something from the past and continued to portray herself as the victim. My mother showed no compassion or empathy for me.

I don't know why I was so surprise at my mother's lack of empathy. When I lost my job, feeling at an all- time low, I went to my mother for comfort. When I told her I was laid off from my job, she had a smile on her face and when my younger sister had a miscarriage she also went to my mother for comfort, but was shocked when my mother burst out laughing.

Empathy; It's how you can "walk a mile in someone else's shoes;" know where they're coming from, and in turn, generate empathy. People that lack empathy are not in-tune with their emotions and put their needs above others. They can't connect with others, understand their experiences and respond with compassion and kindness. Neuroscientists identifies specific brain areas linked to empathy. If specific brain mechanisms are associated with lack of empathy, can we translate these findings as a mental health disorder? The good news is that research has discovered that people can learn to be more empathetic by consistently making a good-faith attempt to.

Despite my oldest sister being the only family

member who believed my mother should take responsibility for her actions, she faced immediate hostility from other sisters when she spoke up for me. As a result, she never defended me again.

When I shared my repressed childhood memories with one sister, she laughed in my face, saying, "You're not the only one who's been abused."

Another sister told me to leave our mother alone, using profanity, and my brother said, "Thru out my life time I have witness how mama have all ways been there for you, more than any of us. She has never hurt you."

What was so cruel my mother used and manipulated my sister who she abused and my brother who she did not protect from abuse. I believe my siblings who were abused wanted to keep their abuse repressed so they wouldn't have to face pain and suffering. Disassociation is something that many survivors of child abuse come to effortlessly do. By disassociating from the memories, or from the feelings, a survivor is able to preserve a relationship with an abusive parent feeling the abuse didn't matter, but the scars from abuse will show up in your behavior, and that's something you cannot hide.

Adults who endured physical or sexual abuse as children may become abusers themselves or face an increased risk of developing issues like substance abuse, depression, low self-esteem, difficulty forming and maintaining relationships, aggressive behavior, engaging in risky behaviors, and more.

I don't believe my siblings turned against me out of unwavering loyalty to our mother; rather, our family prioritizes maintaining a flawless image. The underlying message seems to be that we must project an appearance of perfection, not about right or wrong, but driven by common fears such as "What would the neighbors think?" "What would the relatives think?" and "What would our friends think?" This fear of judgment dictates our family's actions, overshadowing the importance of addressing the abuse and seeking justice.

It's crucial not to be afraid to speak out about abuse. Your voice is one of the most powerful instruments in the human body. Isaiah 58:1 encourages us to use our voices: "Cry aloud, spare not, lift up thy voice like a trumpet, and shew my people their transgression."

Opening up about abuse caused by a family member can be challenging, but sharing your story is an essential part of the healing process. Don't allow others to silence your voice with gaslighting, aggression, manipulation, humiliation, and intimidation;

these are forms of emotional abuse. Stand firm in expressing your truth and seek the support you need.

Tell your story—shout it, write it, whisper it if you have to, but tell it. Some may not understand, others might outright reject it, but many will thank you for sharing. And then, the most magical thing will happen: one by one, voices will start whispering, "Me, too." This shared experience will give someone the extra shot of courage they need to embark on their own journey of speaking, healing, and bringing darkness to light.

When hurt occurs in family relationships, it's beneficial to go through a process of relationship healing, bringing all parties involved together, offering apologies, and granting forgiveness.

My intention was not to expose family secrets to the world. Instead, I hoped for my family to show love and compassion, but their attempts to silence me only fueled my determination to speak out.

Psalms 7:15-16 remind us, "They dig a hole to trap others, but they will fall into it themselves. They will get themselves into trouble; the violence they cause will hurt only themselves." In seeking truth and healing, it's essential to confront the issues rather than perpetuate a cycle of harm.

CHAPTER 9
Contemplating Suicide

After I left my job, I stayed with my cousin for two months. During that time, I found a new job, but I didn't have enough money to get my own place. When I left my cousin's house, I had to move into a shelter for women and children. I stayed there for about four months.

After leaving the shelter, I spent the Christmas holidays with my daughter, her husband, and my grandkids. They didn't know I was homeless. When I expressed concern about my son-in-law being too harsh in disciplining my grandson, he asked me to leave their house. My daughter got me a hotel room for the night, thinking I was still staying with my cousin. I told her that my cousin had company over for the holidays, so I needed to find somewhere else to stay.

Now, that voice in my head that has always told me my life had valve was gone. I started reflecting on how unloved I've felt throughout my life and all the hardships I've faced. This led me to feel like I was in a deep dark hole with no light, and that's when I realized I no longer wanted to live. I felt ashamed to share my suicidal thoughts with my daughter.

When you're going through a tough time, the pain can become so overwhelming that ending your life may seem like the only way to stop it. Thoughts of suicide can cloud your mind, making it hard to think clearly. You may feel a sense of hopelessness and shame for even having such thoughts. It's crucial to be around people and reach out to someone who can help lift you out of that darkness.

During that particularly difficult moment, my daughter rented a hotel room for me, accompanied by my grandkids. As I waited for them to leave, I had planned to take sleeping pills to end my life. However, they stayed with me throughout the night, preventing me from carrying out my plan. Unable to act with them there, I went to sleep feeling utterly hopeless about my homeless situation. To this day, my daughter remains unaware that her decision to stay with me at the hotel that night saved my life. Reflecting on this experience, I am reminded of a scripture that says, "Weeping may endure for a night, but joy cometh in the morning" (Psalm 30:5).

That's exactly what happened to me. When I woke up the next morning, I started pulling myself out of that deep, dark place. I began to see a faint glimmer of hope, and the voice in my head that always reminded me my life had value was slowly returning. That's when I realized I wanted to keep living.

Even though I walk through the darkest valley, I will fear no evil, for you are with me; your rod and your staff, they comfort me. (Psalm 23:4).

If you're thinking about suicide and feeling hopeless, please hold on, I promise things will get better. As it says in Isaiah 40:31, But those who wait on the LORD shall renew their strength; They shall mount up with wings like eagles, They shall run and not be weary, They shall walk and not faint.

Psalm 92:12 says, "The righteous shall flourish like the palm tree."

In storms, palm trees can bend a lot, almost touching the ground, but they don't break. When the storm passes, they stand tall again. Scientists have found that after a storm, the palm tree is even stronger than before. After checking out of the hotel with nowhere to stay, I spent a night in my car, realizing I couldn't live like that. Determined to keep going, I asked my aunt if I could stay with her. I stayed there for a month until the opportunity for a townhouse came up. Despite being told there was a one-year waiting list, after just four months, I moved into my townhouse. It felt like a blessing from God, and I was incredibly grateful.

Whenever my thoughts dwell on what I've lost and the challenges I've faced, I shift my focus to thanking God for my blessings. This transition from grief to gratitude helps me find a more positive perspective.

Expressing gratitude intentionally directs my thoughts toward things that bring joy. Studies show that practicing gratitude can positively impact brain chemistry, influencing how the brain functions and, consequently, affecting our overall quality of life.

Learning to manage thoughts and behaviors to optimize the brain's chemistry is a worthwhile effort for a better and more fulfilling life.

CHAPTER 10
Why Does God Allow Suffering?

God did not bring pain and suffering into the world. According to Genesis 1:31, God saw everything He had made as good. When God created humans, He granted them free will, allowing them to make their own choices. The Scriptures explain that suffering entered the world due to the sins of Adam and Eve. As a result of sin, God brought judgment upon the earth, leading to suffering, pain, disease, sorrow, and death.

The Bible mentions that women undergo intense labor pains during childbirth as a consequence of Eve's sin. Genesis 3:16 states, "To the women He said, 'I will make your pains in childbearing very severe; with painful labor you will give birth to children.'"

It's natural to question God during difficult times. For instance, when facing abuse as a child, one may wonder why God did not protect them. Why does God let children suffer? When God flooded the earth, He saved Noah and his family, but what about the kids who perished because of their parents' wrongdoing?

In the case of Sodom and Gomorrah, God destroyed the cities due to sin. Only Lot and his family were rescued, leaving us to wonder why innocent children had to suffer for the sins of others.

The Bible in Isaiah 55:8-9 says, "My thoughts are not like your thoughts, and my ways are different from yours," declares the LORD. This means that God's ways are beyond our understanding, just as the heavens are higher than the earth.

When Jesus walked the earth he was fully human, He struggled with the need to accept suffering. In praying, "Let this cup pass from me. The "cup" to which Jesus refers is the suffering He was about to endure. The crucifixion of Christ was brutal. He was beaten with His hands and feet nailed to a rough plank of wood. A crown make with thorns was rammed onto His head, causing blood to gush down His face. In a moment of deep anguish on the cross, Jesus cried out loudly, "My God, My God, why have You forsaken Me?" (Matthew 27:46) This cry reveals a moment of questioning and distress, as Jesus sought to understand why God allowed him to undergo such intense suffering. It reflects a profound human experience where even Jesus, on a mission to redeem the world, momentarily felt forsaken and struggled with faith.

This aspect of Jesus' journey emphasizes the

depth of his humanity and the emotional challenges he faced, making his sacrifice and ultimate victory even more significant in Christian beliefs.

The Bible advises, "Beloved, don't be surprised by the difficult challenges you face, as if something strange is happening. When you share in the sufferings of Christ, rejoice, so that when His glory is revealed, you may rejoice with great joy" (1 Peter 4:12 -13). Similarly, in James 1:2-4, it encourages believers to find joy in facing various trials because the testing of faith develops perseverance. The goal is for perseverance to lead to maturity and completeness.

During times of suffering when understanding may be elusive, there's a caution against turning away from God. The enemy might tempt you to do so, but the counsel is to trust in God despite the uncertainties. This reflects a message of resilience, perseverance, and trust in God's greater purpose even in the face of adversity. The Bible encourages us, saying, "Trust in the Lord with all your heart, and do not rely on your own understanding. In all your ways acknowledge Him, and He will make your paths straight" (Proverbs 3:5-6).

When you place your trust in God, hope becomes a powerful force that helps you overcome your past and look toward a brighter future. Hope enables you to face each day with determination and strengthens your faith in God. With hope, fears can be cast aside because hope is more greater than fear.

Jesus, through His sacrificial life, provided a way for humanity to be saved from the consequences of sin. The Bible emphasizes that salvation comes exclusively through Jesus Christ (John 14:6). Jesus is not merely one option among many; He is the singular path to salvation.

By following the example set by Jesus, who made a way for us to be in God's presence and live in Heaven, we can find purpose in our lives. While we may not be able to make the same sacrifices as Jesus, if we extend compassion to others who are suffering, saving one life at a time, our lives gain greater meaning even in the midst of our own suffering.

CHAPTER 11
Emotional Detachment

After seeing pictures of my mom on Facebook, it was really sad to see her looking old and fragile. I felt guilty for not visiting her, so for her birthday, I got her a gift. When I went to see her, she didn't look at me and kept her head down the whole time, like she was going through something like dementia. I wanted to tell her that I didn't hold any grudges for how she treated me and that I understood she did her best for us, her children. My brother was also there, so I couldn't say those things to her.

My heart ached for my mother, a beautiful woman who didn't have the life she deserved. She endured verbal and physical abuse, leading to an unhappy life filled with disappointments. Due to low self-esteem and a lack of understanding of her self-worth, she never received the mental help needed for a better life. Some women, especially those who have faced abuse and childhood difficulties, struggle with control over their lives, resulting in low self-esteem. Unfortunately, they may even project their insecurities onto their own children.

As I left my mother's apartment in the retirement home, I couldn't shake the feeling that it might be the last time I would see her alive, and I feared I would never have another chance to mend our relationship.

Concerned, I reached out to my oldest sister to inquire about our mother's health. She reassured me that our mother was not sick and was in good health. This led me to speculate that perhaps my mother's inability to look at me stemmed from shame for her actions or perhaps she still saw herself as a victim.

My mother never personally apologized or expressed remorse; instead, family members would call to guilt-trip me. I only confronted my mother once about not protecting me when I was a child, but for years, she cried victim because I was not giving her recognition and praise she desired. It seemed like she was seeking solace, hoping I would let go and forgive. However, after years of trying to avoid blaming her for the consequences of her actions, I felt exhausted and mentally drained. Despite her fragile self-esteem, I consistently gave her the recognition, praise, and admiration she craved.

In my efforts to build her up, I allowed my mother to beat me down emotionally. I continued acknowledging her on special occasions like her birthday, Mother's Day, and even Valentine's Day. In doing so, I realized I was following the pattern of my siblings who had also been abused – disassociating from the painful memories to maintain a relationship with our mother.

Eventually, I had to accept that when a mother doesn't love you, there is nothing you can do to make her love you.

Narcissistic mothers' love is conditional, depending on whether their children are acting in accordance with their entitled expectations and needs.

Daughters of narcissistic mothers are grieving a relationship that they never had and will never have. They're mourning for a relationship that's absent whether their mother is alive or not. These daughters often have to face ambiguous loss, which is the grief of losing a relationship that never was or no longer is without a clear understanding or closure.

In her nineties, my mother continued to cause me pain by turning my siblings against me, portraying herself as the victim and victimizing me once again. Some may question how a ninety-year-old woman could hurt anyone. A ninety-year old woman can't physically hurt you, but my ninety-year-old mother was able to manipulate and turn my siblings against me with lies, ultimately causing me to lose the love and respect of my family.

It's a reminder of the power of words. The

tongue holds incredible power, capable of bringing blessings or curses. Psalms 34:13 advises to keep one's tongue from evil and lips from telling lies.

The Bible also cautions against actions that the Lord detests, including a lying tongue and one who sows discord among brothers, as mentioned in Proverbs 6:16-19: "There are six things that the LORD hates, seven that are an abomination to him: haughty eyes, a lying tongue, and hands that shed innocent blood, a heart that devises wicked plans, feet that make haste to run to evil, a false witness who breathes out lies, and one who sows discord among brothers." These verses highlight the importance of truthfulness and avoiding actions that lead to division and harm.

I recall the moment I confided in my aunt, my father's sister, about the ordeal my mother put me through when I was just 16. Over the phone, I couldn't hold back my tears, conveying the profound impact it had on me. Surprisingly, my aunt displayed more compassion for my mother than for me, her own blood relative.

She said, "Nothing could stop me from wanting to see my mother." That response prompted me to research why I felt so emotionally detached from a mother who I loved. I came to understand that emotional detachment from someone who has abused you is not a reflection of your love for that person. Rather, it serves as a coping mechanism to shield yourself from further hurt. I recognized a pattern in my life of emotionally detaching myself from people as a means of self-protection.

To overcome emotional detachment, I consciously surrounded myself with individuals whom I felt safe with. Building stronger emotional attachments became possible when I sensed that a person genuinely had my best interests at heart.

Throughout my life I've been resilience having the ability to cope and recover from being knock down so many times, but everything can run its course. I had to realize both aspects of being resilience are intertwined with being vulnerable and acknowledging my needs and limitations and knowing I need help by finding my own pathway to healing.

CHAPTER 12

Cutting Family Ties

For five years, my daughter, grandkids, and I were estranged from most family members, with the exception of my oldest sister. Estrangement involves a broken or disrupted family relationship where communication and interaction are reduced or ceased.

The Bible advises us in Hebrews 12:14 to "Make every effort to live in peace with everyone and to be holy; without holiness, no one will see the Lord." However, reconciling with family can be a challenging journey, and a family rift is one of the most traumatic experiences one can face. This situation can significantly impact mental health. Nevertheless, if attempts at making amends prove unsuccessful, it becomes necessary to accept the decision and find a way to move forward, accepting the reality of the situation.

It's crucial to recognize that estrangement doesn't always have an exclusively negative impact on those involved. For some, cutting off communication and distancing from a perceived toxic family member can lead to decreased stress, increased insight, self-understanding, and feelings of strength and happiness after severing negative ties. It's acceptable to remove people from your life, even if they are family, if they don't love or respect you. Despite societal pressures that may make you feel like something is wrong with you, there's no need to feel ashamed or guilty about not having a relationship with family members who don't show love or respect.

However, if your desire is to reconnect with estranged family members and repair the relationship, it's usually a gradual process rather than a single event that allows time for reconciliation. Reconciliation can become impossible if the person who caused hurt refuses to apologize or if both sides don't make the effort to reconnect. It's important to prioritize your well-being and make decisions that contribute to your mental and emotional health.

As businesses gradually reopened following the initial lockdowns from the pandemic, my family began hosting holiday and birthday parties. However, when my daughter took the brave step to reconnect with some family members after being estranged for five years, she faced rejection from certain relatives. Personally, I chose not to reconnect with my family because I recognized their toxicity. I found contentment in simply being with my daughter and grandkids, enjoying a drama-free and happy life together.

The only sister I maintained communication with was my oldest sister, with whom I had a strong relationship. Occasionally, she would extend invitations to my daughter, grandkids, and me to join her for holiday gatherings at her house. I continued to support my oldest sister, who suffers from multiple sclerosis, by assisting her when she moved into her new home. I helped with cleaning, cooking, and during the Christmas season, I took on tasks such as decorating her Christmas tree, doing her shopping, and accompanying her for holiday meal preparations. My commitment to helping my sister demonstrated the depth of our bond and my willingness to support her in any way possible.

After Christmas, I attached my oldest sister's wheelchair to the car, and we went shopping for post-Christmas sales to buy materials for making Christmas wreaths. The plan was for me to teach her how to decorate wreaths, with the goal of selling them during the next Christmas season. We even discussed the possibility of creating a website to showcase and sell the wreaths we would craft together. Additionally, my oldest sister expressed an interest in learning how to sew, so I promised to take her to sewing classes twice a week to help her acquire this skill. My intention was to contribute to improving her quality of life.

However, our plans were disrupted by the onset of the pandemic, preventing us from continuing with our projects. As word spread among my other sisters about the assistance I was providing to our oldest sister, they began visiting her as well, attempting to show love despite their infrequent visits.

Unfortunately my sisters were able to manipulate my oldest sister by targeting her weaknesses, giving her the attention she craved from not receiving love and attention as a child. Instead of considering their character, my oldest sister focused on what my five sisters could do for her.

It's easy to be impressed by what a person can do for you: their income, social status, or job title. But do they show the same courtesy and respect to all? How do they make other people, especially those who are different from them, feel about themselves? When choosing a friend, mate, or the right political candidate, remember Philippians 4:8, "Finally, brothers and sisters, whatever is true, whatever is noble, whatever is right, whatever is pure, whatever is lovely, whatever is admirable—if anything is excellent or praiseworthy—think about such things".

Surprisingly, my oldest sister didn't believe she

needed my help. When I questioned her stepdaughter, who was her care provider, about the quality of care she was providing, my sister's husband asked me to leave their home at my sister's request. This situation highlighted the complexities and challenges of family dynamics, particularly during times of adversity.

It was disheartening when my oldest sister jumped on the bandwagon, treating me the same as the other family members who had distanced themselves from me. The bandwagon effect, recognized as a form of manipulation, aims to influence people to join in with the majority, creating an assumption that if many others are doing something, it must be good or at least acceptable. Unfortunately, this approach doesn't allow individuals to assess their own values and beliefs to determine if the prevailing trend aligns with their choices.

The bandwagon effect often prompts people to conform to the actions or beliefs of others, seeking approval and a sense of fitting in. One significant mistake my oldest sister made was sharing with the other sisters the help I was providing her. This disclosure led to the deterioration of our relationship, and they, in turn, deprived her of the blessings she was receiving from my assistance.

Following the manipulation by my other sisters, who turned her against me, they later abandoned her when she needed help. Living with multiple sclerosis and reliant on a wheelchair, my oldest sister required assistance when her husband was hospitalized. However, my sisters couldn't bring themselves to stay overnight at her house, perhaps considering it beneath them. This situation highlighted the consequences of their actions and the fragility of relationships within the family.

It was a poignant moment when none of my sisters offered to stay overnight and help my oldest sister, who was in need, but my daughter and teenage grandson stepped up to the plate and stayed the night to assist her.

Maya Angelou, the esteemed American poet, author, and civil rights activist, once wisely said, "When someone shows you who they are, believe them the first time." In this case, my sisters' actions, or lack thereof, reflected their priorities and true selves. Their indifference towards my oldest sister was evident when she lived in a small two-bedroom duplex, struggling to move around in her wheelchair. It wasn't until she moved into her new house that my sisters suddenly showed interest.

The dynamics within my family were characterized by constant comparisons of achievements and a tendency to look down on certain family members. This ongoing behavior provided a clear insight into the nature of their relationships and priorities.

Despite the strained dynamics, my younger sister attempted to mend our relationship. However, when I allowed her back into my life, it became apparent that her intentions were not centered on rebuilding our connection. Instead, she brought up a past source of conflict by informing me that I was not invited to a family gathering at another sister's house because I would likely choose not to attend. This revelation signaled that her focus was more on maintaining division than fostering reconciliation.

It's ironic that my sister, who had experienced rejection herself, would not empathize with my feelings. Having once faced exclusion from our mother and other sisters when she didn't align with the majority. She had expressed the profound pain and impact of the being rejection by the family and how the abuse she endured during her childhood had affected her life.

I get why my sister couldn't show love or care when our family rejected me. As a kid, she never experienced love or compassion herself. She acts tough, but deep down, she's fragile, using that toughness to shield herself from getting hurt.

When my oldest sister's husband passed away, despite how she treated me, I put aside my hurt and called to offer condolences and support. She was scared to be alone at night and had nightmares, yet none of my sisters had the heart to stay overnight with her after her loss.

For over twenty years, our family tradition included holiday sleepovers. However, my sisters made excuses to avoid staying overnight at my oldest sister's house during her grieving period. My oldest sister reached out, asking if I could stay with her three nights a week. I agreed. Initially, it was tough for me to push aside my hurt and anger, as I wished for an apology from her. However, I understood she was grieving, so I focused on supporting her instead of making it about myself.

To bring joy to my sister during the tough time of losing her husband close to the holidays, I decorated her Christmas tree and home, spending the holidays with her. On Christmas day, my sisters didn't reach out to her, aware it was her first Christmas without her husband. I was there for her when no one else was.

When my oldest sister confronted the other sisters about not including me on the family group texts letting me know about sickness and deaths in the family, she was met with anger and hostility, so to fit in with the majority, again she jumped on the bandwagon, turning against me. I felt betrayed. It felt like déjà vu. I was experiencing the same thing over again. I never wanted my oldest sister to defend me, because I knew she would be cast aside from the family. My younger sister, who has a tough exterior due to childhood abuse, claimed I wasn't included in family group texts because I explicitly expressed a desire not to be.

The group text messages my sister referred to were not related to family emergencies; rather, my sisters were using them to discuss personal matters and engage in arguments. I chose not to be included in those conversations, as they didn't concern family issues. My sister knew I was not talking about not being notified about family emergencies. I didn't harbor anger; instead, I empathized with my sister, recognizing that individuals in pain may seek to inflict it on others as a way of feeling powerful.

Reflecting on the situation, I considered the potential harm that negativity could cause within a family. I recalled the guidance from the Bible: "Make no friendship with a person given to anger, nor go with a person full of hate, lest you learn their ways and entangle yourself in a trap" (Proverbs 22:24-25). This wisdom influenced my decision to maintain healthy boundaries and avoid getting entangled in destructive dynamics.

If you have a compassionate heart and wish to extend mercy to someone who has wronged you, it's important to safeguard your emotions. Trying to rebuild a relationship with someone who doesn't value you or refuses to acknowledge their wrongdoing may not be the healthiest choice.

As I begin to study family relationships I learned children first learn how to love from their parents. Parents who show love and affection for each other teach their children how to love. Children are mirrors, reflecting images of what happens around them. So I realized my sibling and I am a product of growing up in a family with physical and emotional abuse where love was rarely shown. The bible tells us anyone can change." Therefore, if anyone is in Christ, the new creation has come: The old has gone, the new is here!" (2 Corinthians 5:17).

Sometimes, despite the desire for change, if your family chooses not to evolve and no longer holds love or respect for you, it becomes necessary to let go and move forward. Love and respect act as the essential bonds that keep relationships intact, and when they are absent, relationships may crumble.

Recognizing toxicity is crucial, even if it originates within your own family. It's okay to distance yourself from people who consistently inflict harm on you. Your relatives, members of your own family— even they have betrayed you; they have raised a loud cry against you. Do not trust them. (Jeremiah 12:6)

Put your Faith and Trust in God, "So that your faith might not rest in the wisdom of men but in the power of God". (1 Corinthians 2:5)

This approach can provide a foundation for resilience and guidance as one navigates challenging family dynamics.

CHAPTER 13

Another Layer of Trauma

My daughter started giving me journals and asked me to share my life story. When she noticed I wasn't interested, she began posting details about my life on social media. Family members shared inaccurate information about my pregnancy with her. When I asked her to stop, she insisted, saying, "You need to tell your story so you won't be misrepresented." This motivated me to write a book.

It hurts that my family, who claim to be Christians, would share things that could harm my daughter and damage our relationship. They knew the impact on her emotional state and deliberately manipulated her. It's disheartening that they would turn a daughter against her mother.

The Bible, in Titus 1:16, states, "They claim to know God, but they deny him by what they do. They are detestable, disobedient, and unfit to do anything good."

I anticipated that my daughter would eventually learn about the circumstances of her conception. However, I now regret sharing the truth with her, especially as she was already grappling with her own challenges. Surprisingly, she turned against me, downplaying my experiences of abuse, much like other family members. It is difficult to comprehend the lack of compassion or empathy towards someone who endured childhood abuse. Sadly, no one in my family expressed empathy for what happened to me; instead, they turned against me when I spoke out about my past.

Receiving an email from my daughter defending my mother (her grandmother), and her father who had nothing to do with her, the man who took advantage of me added another layer of trauma for me. My daughter took what happen to me personally. It was not about her. Although she was conceived from painful memories, she was loved and brought joy to our family.

As an unwed teenage mother with no child support and bleak prospects, I worked hard to ensure my daughter and I had health and life insurance. Despite the challenges, I was never a neglectful mother. I remained actively involved in my daughter's life. When my daughter got married and had children, I was in a position to provide support.

For over 20 years, I dedicated my life to helping my daughter raise her children. I picked up my grandkids from school daily, cooked nutritious meals, and created a loving, safe environment for them. My daughter often expressed her gratitude through greeting cards and Facebook posts, acknowledging the support I provided to her family.

Face book posts;
"Always praying that my Mom has a truly Blessed Birthday!!! We appreciate all of the love, support, and care she gives our family!!! We hope you enjoyed your celebration, because we love celebrating you!!!

"Everyone please wish my Mom a very Happy Birthday!!!!

My Mom is beautiful, creative, giving to others, & enjoys being of service to children & her elders. I am eternally grateful for God allowing you to give me life. That was the most important blessing of my life. For that Ultimate sacrifice, I will be forever grateful. Praying that you felt truly Blessed & loved from us. We Love You!!!"

"A mother's love is a priceless treasured gift. Throughout your life, many relationships evolve and grow, but your first & most intimate relationship begins with your mother. Without your Mom, you have no possibility to exist. So I thank God everyday that you chose to be my Mom."

"Girl Scouts Mother & Daughter Tea was Fabulous according to my Mom. I feel blessed to have my Mom to take my daughter to special events when I can't. Team work makes the dream work!!! Thanks a MILLION Mom!!!"

Despite the years of love and support I provided to my daughter and her family, she began disrespecting and trying to hurt me. My sisters took advantage of her vulnerabilities, manipulating her into thinking they would offer love and support, making her believe she didn't need me. However, after they disrupted the family unit I had with my daughter and grandkids, most of the family rejected her once again.

On Mother's Day, my daughter did not acknowledge me; instead, she had my grandkids express their acknowledgment. Additionally, when I received an invitation to her birthday celebration, it was addressed to Nana, not Mom, signaling her reluctance to address me as her mother.

During one Christmas holiday, my daughter went out of town, taking my grandkids with her, seemingly to hurt me. It was a painful experience as I had never missed celebrating Christmas with them before. The hurt and loneliness I felt were indescribable.

I came to understand that loneliness doesn't stem from being alone; it arises from feeling that nobody cares. With no family or friends to spend the holidays with, I found myself back in a dark hole. The burden of being strong and resilient became overwhelming, and I was tired of suppressing traumatic memories just to survive.

In a moment of despair, I cried out to God, questioning why I wasn't allowed to die in that hotel room. Feeling like I had nothing to live for, my grandkids unexpectedly called me, saying, "Merry Christmas Nana, I love you!" Those words brought a glimmer of hope and reminded me that, even in my darkest moments, there was still love and connection worth living for.

It felt like I had been carried a hundred miles away from the shore, surrounded by nothing but water, with only two arm floaties to keep me from drowning. In that moment, I clung to those floaties until I was rescued and back on solid ground. My two grandkids became my lifeline, providing joy and happiness during lonely and challenging times.

Despite the hardships, my grandkids have always been a source of unconditional love, and I am grateful to my daughter for giving me such a precious gift. They were my beacon of hope during those tough moments. If you just look around, you can always find something to be thankful for, and that will give you hope."

As Oprah Winfrey wisely said, "Be thankful for what you have, you'll end up having more. If you concentrate on what you don't have you will never, ever have enough"

Life is filled with continuous trials, as we are told to expect. However, the comforting news is that we don't have to face these trials alone. I prayed to God, asking Him to remind me to be thankful even in the midst of great adversity.

In response, God provided the strength and peace I needed to navigate through the holidays and future occasions when I might find myself alone. I discovered the importance of finding my own joy by identifying things that make me happy and bring me joy. This realization allowed me to face challenges with a renewed perspective and a sense of inner strength.

CHAPTER 14
Forgiveness

It can be especially painful when hurt comes from within your own family. Unlike friends or co-workers, families are expected to be close-knit and loyal. When you share your pain with family, the response may be anger or dismissal, with comments like, "Why can't you let that go?" This can minimize your hurt and abuse, dictating how you should feel without any acknowledgment or apology.

Apologizing is a crucial part of seeking humility, a quality highly valued by God. The power of apologizing can restore relationships, ease conflicts, and aid in letting go and moving forward. The Bible emphasizes not harboring hatred within your heart for relatives and encourages direct confrontation to avoid being held guilty for their wrongs (Leviticus 19:17). This approach promotes accountability and facilitates healing within family relationships.

Psychologists typically define forgiveness as a conscious, deliberate decision to let go of feelings of resentment or vengeance towards someone who has harmed you, regardless of whether they deserve your forgiveness. However, the question arises: should we forgive without an apology?

Forgiving without an apology can be challenging, as a genuine apology is often seen as a crucial step in healing a broken relationship. Without acknowledgment and remorse from the person who caused harm, the relationship may remain strained. Forgiving someone who hurt you without receiving an apology may not benefit anyone involved.

So often we make the victim feel guilty about not forgiving the person who refuses to ask for forgiveness, releasing them from the responsibilities of their actions.

The complexity of forgiveness involves a delicate balance between personal healing, accountability, and the restoration of relationships.

Letting go of grudges to release feeling like a victim so you'll no longer define your life by how you've been hurt has nothing to do with forgiving a person who refuses to ask for forgiveness.

You pray for those who persecute you. (Matthew 5:44). You ask God what is written in, Psalm 51:10, God create in me a clean heart, O God, and renew a right spirit within me"

So when you hold a person responsible for their behavior, the intent is to promote another person's well-being to bring them closer to God.

He that takes an ingenuous liberty to tell others

of their faults, and rebukes them freely, when need requires, to their face, is a better friend. (Proverbs 27:5-6)

Holding a person accountable for their behavior is not about seeking revenge but promoting their well-being and guiding them closer to God. The Bible, in James 5:20, encourages turning a sinner from their ways to save them from death and cover a multitude of sins. The underlying motivation here is love. Love has the power to diminish hurt and pain, freeing you from the burden of feeling like a victim. By focusing on love, one can find healing and move towards a path of renewal and spiritual well-being.

If the person who has caused you harm shows no interest in repairing the relationship, The Bible tell us in Matthew 18:15-17, " If your brother sins against you, go and tell him his fault, between you and him alone. If he listens to you, you have gained your brother. But if he does not listen, let him be to you as a Gentile and a tax collector. Gentiles and Tax Collectors reject the Gospel message of Jesus and live according to their own desires and knowledge. Moving on with your life can bring relief, offering a welcome sense of freedom and peace.

However, if someone genuinely seeks forgiveness, the Bible commands us to forgive. Biblical forgiveness is understood as God's promise not to count our sins against us. A crucial condition for receiving forgiveness from God is our willingness to forgive others. As stated in Matthew 6:14-15, "For if you forgive other people when they sin against you, your heavenly Father will also forgive you. But if you do not forgive others their sins, your Heavenly Father will not forgive your sins." This emphasizes the reciprocal nature of forgiveness, linking our forgiveness of others to God's forgiveness of our own sins.

The bible tells us to forgive those who sin against us, but do we forgive those who refused to apologize who have sinned against us? The Bible says; "Take heed to yourselves: If thy brother trespass against thee, REBUKE him; and if he RE-PENT, forgive him; And if he sins against you seven time in a day, and seven time in a day returns to you, saying, "I repent, "you shall forgive him. Luke 17:3-4. It's crucial to note the conjunction "and" in the passage, emphasizing the sequence of actions: first, rebuke, and then, if the person repents, forgive.

The Bible teaches a balanced approach that involves honest communication, rebuke when needed, and forgiveness when genuine repentance is expressed.

So you have these two teachings. Jesus is saying

forgive other people when they sin against you, your heavenly Father will also forgive you, but then Jesus is also saying "Take heed to yourselves: If thy brother trespass against thee, REBUKE him; and if he REPENT, forgive him.

So how do we solve this apparent dilemma?

Jesus teaches by example. I look at how our sins are forgiven when we sin against God.

When you sin against your brethren, and wound their weak conscience, you sin against Christ. (1 Corinthians 8:12)

The Bible provides a clear path for the forgiveness of sins when we transgress against Christ. Acts 3:19 states, "Repent, then, and turn to God, so that your sins may be wiped out, that times of refreshing may come from the Lord."

Sin creates a separation between us and God, as indicated in Isaiah 59:2: "But your iniquities have made a separation between you and your God, and your sins have hidden his face from you so that he does not hear." Repentance is the key to restoring that connection with God.

God's love is unconditional, and He doesn't hold grudges when we fail to repent. Romans 5:8 affirms this by stating, "But God shows his love for us in that while we were still sinners, Christ died for us."

Even in our sinful state, God's love remains stead-fast.

Confessing our sins is a crucial part of the process. As mentioned in 1 John 1:9, "If we confess our sins, God is faithful and will forgive us our sins and cleanse us from all unrighteousness." This underscores the importance of acknowledging our wrongs and seeking forgiveness through repentance and confession.

The Bible Story of Joseph and his brothers from the Book of Genesis shows us true repentance, remorse, and renewal.

The story of Joseph illustrates a powerful example of forgiveness. Despite facing hatred and betrayal from his own brothers, who initially plotted to kill him and later sold him into slavery, Joseph eventually rose to a position of power in Egypt. When his brothers, unaware that Joseph was alive and well, came to him seeking help, Joseph had the opportunity for revenge. However, instead of seeking retribution, he chose forgiveness and reconciliation.

Joseph's ability to forgive reflects a profound understanding of God's greater plan, even in times of suffering. Similarly, in our own lives, we are called to forgive those who genuinely seek forgiveness and to view life's experiences as part of God's overarching plan. This perspective allows for healing, reconciliation, and the possibility of contributing to a greater good, just as Joseph's forgiveness played a crucial role in the larger narrative of God's plan.

CHAPTER 15

The Power of Prayer

Prayer is possible because Jesus Christ has removed the barrier between us and God—a barrier caused by our sins. But by His death on the cross, Christ paid the penalty for our sins and removed the barrier. The power of prayer is our means of communication with God, allowing us to seek His guidance and assistance on our life journey. Through prayer, we surrender our lives to God, trusting that He will lead us along the path He has planned for us. It is essential to teach our children the importance of prayer from an early age.

Matthew 6-9-13 gives us an example on how to pray. Address Heavenly Father, ask for forgiveness of sins, thank Him for blessings, ask Him for blessings, close in the name of <u>Jesus Christ</u>.

As Matthew 6:6 suggests, when we pray, we should enter a private space, shut the door, and communicate with our Father who sees in secret. This emphasizes the intimate and personal nature of prayer, and the promise that God, who sees our hearts, will reward our sincerity. Prayer also teaches us to consider the needs of others before our own, as highlighted in James 4:3. It reminds us that self-centered or misguided prayers may not align with God's will.

Philippians 4:6 encourages us not to worry but to present our requests to God through prayer, supplication, and thanksgiving. This verse underscores the power of prayer in alleviating anxieties and fostering a sense of gratitude.

Hebrews 11:6 emphasizes that faith is crucial in pleasing God. It requires belief in God's existence and trust that He rewards those who earnestly seek Him.

First, realize that sometimes God is actually answering our prayers when we don't realize it. His answer may be "No" or "Wait." Yes, we think we know what's best for us—but God sees the whole picture, and sometimes He lovingly refuses to give us what we request, because He knows it isn't according to His perfect plan.

My personal testimony reflects a deep sense of pain and rejection. I can testify God does answer prayers. I was feeling broken from being rejected by my family, church members and every organization I tried to join that knew my passion for helping children. And no matter how much I tried to be a blessing to whomever I met, I was constantly being rejected, and that constant rejection felt like hate and it caused me to have rejection sensitivity which almost broke me.

I cried out to God, "God please help me to find a Church congregation of loving, kind, God-fearing people so I can have a family. Although my grandkids loved me unconditionally, with almost my entire family being against me, the world seemed so small.

Not only did God help me a find a loving , kind, God-fearing congregation of people, but He send me a loving kind, God-fearing friend who has been there for me when I needed a shoulder to cry on.

Your acknowledgment of the challenges in the world and the importance of seeking God's protection through praycr reflect a realistic and humble perspective. We are living in an evil and dangerous world, but some of us go through life never expecting bad things to happen. We think that we are invincible with a hedge of protection around us, protecting us from the bad things of this world, but we need to pray every day to ask God to surround us with His presence, and put our lives in His hands.

"But the Lord is faithful, and he will strengthen

you and protect you from the evil one". (2 Thessalonians 3:3).

Therefore humble yourselves under the reassurance that Jesus can remove heavy burdens, such as guilt and hopelessness, aligns with the comforting and redemptive aspect of faith.

It encourages believers to find true rest in Him, acknowledging that through prayer and trust in God, burdens can be lifted and a sense of peace can be attained.

CHAPTER 16

Finding Happiness in Christ

Happiness is an emotional state of well-being defined by positive or pleasant emotions ranging from contentment to intense joy. I believed like most people that the pursuit of happiness comes from having wreath, material things are having great relationships, but those things will result in temporary happiness, then we end up disappointed and unhappy.

God didn't promise us our lives will always be happy without pain, struggles, and hardships. He promises to give us the strength to get through them.

Philippians 4:11-13 tells us Paul achieved contentment and happiness no matter what situation he faced in life because of his belief in Christ. The Bible tells us; "Set your minds on things that are above, not on things that are on earth" (Colossians 3:2). We work most of our lives, so when we retire we can enjoy our golden years, but so many people never live long enough to reach retirement.

Why, you do not even know what will happen tomorrow. What is your life? You are a mist that appears for little while and then vanishes. (James 4:14)

But our citizenship is in heaven, and from it we await a Savior, the Lord Jesus Christ, who will transform our lowly body to be like his glorious body, by the power that enables him even to subject all things to himself". (Philippians 3:20-2).

Most people believe in the almighty God, the creator of man, but it doesn't seem like most people seek God's word on how they should live in this world. But the word of the Lord remains forever." And this is the word that was preached to you. (1 Peter 1:25) If the word of the Lord remains forever, no man can take away God's word, so why do we look to the wisdom of man to guide us through our spiritual life?

Anyone can be a Bible Scholar (Advanced studies of the Bible). If any of you lacks wisdom, let him ask God, who gives generously to all without reproach, and it will be given him. (James 1:5)

Ask and it will be given to you; seek and you will find; knock and the door will be opened to you. For everyone who asks receives; the one who seeks finds; and to the one who knocks, the door will be opened. (Matthew 7:7-8)

Jesus is the Savior of the world and a perfect example for us. When we follow His teachings, we discover more peace and happiness in life.

While on Earth, Jesus didn't act like he was better than others. Instead, he led by serving. He washed his disciples' feet, fed thousands, visited the sick, and spent time with those others ignored. Jesus lived a humble life, putting others first. There's evidence that helping others can change our brains in a way that makes us happier.

When I started a non-profit mentoring program for kids I knew I was using my talents for a purpose much greater than myself. It brought me joy to know that I was giving kids the platform they needed to build up their confidence and self-esteem.

When helping others, it's crucial to have the right motivation. Some people assist others for personal gain or recognition. If you volunteer hoping for praise and it doesn't come, you might feel upset or disappointed.

The Bible guides us, saying, "Do nothing out of selfish ambition or vain conceit. Rather, in humility, value others above yourselves, not looking to your own interests but each of you to the interests of others" (Philippians 2:3-5). This emphasizes the importance of selfless service, focusing on the needs of others without seeking personal glory.

True happiness, according to the Bible, is found in realizing that worldly pursuits may not bring lasting joy. It suggests that genuine happiness comes from understanding our identity in Christ. In discovering who we are in Christ, we can attain a deeper, spiritual happiness.

CHAPTER 17

Saying Goodbye to My Mother

When my mom broke her hip and needed surgery, I visited her in the hospital, but she wasn't awake. Little did I know that it would be the last time I saw her alive. I prayed for her healing. Later, I told my younger sister I was willing to assist in taking care of Mom once she was out of the hospital. However, it seemed like I was no longer considered part of the family. I was left out of the family group messages, so I didn't know how Mom was doing. My youngest sister didn't accept my offer to help.

I promised myself that once my mom recovered; she would decide if she wanted to see me. Unfortunately, she passed away a week after leaving the hospital. My youngest sister was aware that Mom had only days to live. She informed other family members, allowing them to say their goodbyes, but excluded me. It was the strongest feeling of hate I had ever experienced. The Bible reminds us, "This is how we know who the children of God are and who the children of the devil are: Anyone who does not do what is right is not God's child, nor is anyone who does not love their brother and sister" (1 John 3:10).

I felt a deep ache in my heart because I didn't have a chance to reconcile with my mother. The grieving process was even harder as my sisters continued to treat me as if I wasn't part of the family. My youngest sister excluded me from the meeting at her house to plan our mother's funeral. She didn't share the program with me or invite me to join the family in the limousine to the funeral. Despite not having any input in the funeral arrangements, I must acknowledge that it was well-organized, and the service itself was beautiful.

At the repast following the funeral, I encountered family members I hadn't seen in years, including a niece and baby nephew I had never met. Some of my nephews, whom I used to babysit, greeted me with smiles and big hugs. It was evident that I had missed out on a lot due to our family conflict. Once again, I discussed our family conflicts with my brother-in-law, who is an Elder of the Church. Unfortunately, he was unwilling to intervene, and it became clear that his wife (my sister) was the primary family member perpetuating the ongoing conflict.

A few months before my mother passed away, my aunt conveyed her message, saying, "Your mother wants you to call her." I hesitated, thinking my mother might be playing the victim again, so I chose not to reach out. Now, I'm haunted by the possibility that she wanted to reconcile. I believe my mother felt remorse for her mistakes and sought peace, but she had people around her encouraging a victim mentality. What she truly needed was healing, which could have brought her peace in her final years. It's disheartening that no one in my family cared enough to guide her towards acknowledging her mistakes, as healing comes from admitting faults: "Admit your faults to one another and pray for each other so that you may be healed" (James 5:16).

The family, thinking that yearly birthday parties were what she needed most, might have missed the deeper need for emotional and spiritual healing. As Isaiah 65:17 suggests, true renewal and healing transcend mere celebrations: "For behold, I create new heavens and a new earth; And the former things will not be remembered or come to mind."

Regardless of our age, the Bible reminds us in 2 Corinthians 5:10 that we will all stand before the judgment seat of Christ, receiving what is due for our actions in this life, whether good or bad. Despite our shortcomings, I believe in God's abundant mercy, especially when we are struggling with our trespasses.

In my prayers, I ask for God's mercy upon my mother's soul. I hope that He will consider the goodness she contributed and recognize the internal battles she faced, even when she couldn't control the demons within. May God's mercy prevail over judgment as we entrust her soul into His compassionate hands.

CHAPTER 18
Never Give Up

We are in a trial that never seems to end. So, when we feel like giving up, remember God is a God of all times; He knows exactly how long our trials will endure, and He will give us the strength we need to get through them if we don't give up.

Let's not grow tired of doing what is good; for in due time we shall reap, if we don't give up. (Galatians 6:9).

I will spend my remaining days on this earth advocating for abused children. I aim to teach children never to allow anyone to make them feel like they are nobody. Always recognize your worth and understand that you count.

Life will inevitably bring both highs and lows, but now I am better equipped to face challenges because the trials I have experienced have made me stronger. With the knowledge I have gained, I cannot overlook the influence of Satan. Satan is acutely aware of human tendencies and exploits that knowledge to target individual weaknesses, making it crucial for us to be vigilant against such influences.

For Satan to gain access to God's people, he may not appear as an obvious threat like a poisonous snake. Instead, he can disguise himself within our own families or among those who claim to be Christians. Using flattering words and a friendly demeanor, he makes it challenging for believers not to be deceived. Regardless of the form he takes, his ultimate goal is to lead people towards destruction.

However, God has equipped us with tools from Scripture, His words, to combat Satan's influence. Ephesians 6:10-11 advises us, "Finally, be strong in the Lord and His mighty power. Put on the full armor of God, so that you can take your stand against the devil's schemes." This emphasizes the importance of relying on God's strength and utilizing the spiritual armor provided in Scripture to resist the deceitful tactics of the devil.

Writing my life story for this book has been the most challenging task I've ever undertaken. Revisiting traumatic memories was extremely stressful, and there were moments when I doubted if I could endure it. Despite knowing that sharing my life story would expose family secrets, I also recognized its potential to help others.

Throughout my life, I have faced abuse, hurt, and pain, resulting in the loss of love and respect from my family. Yet, I wouldn't alter anything about my journey because it has shaped the strong, compassionate, proud, yet humble person I am today. I am committed to being a blessing to those I encounter.

Every morning when I wake up, I affirm to myself, "I'm here, I'm still here!" My survival through abuse, hurt, and pain wasn't achieved by repressing traumatic memories. While the brain has the ability to push such memories aside for coping, it's essential to recognize that repressed memories can resurface, and depending on one's state of mind, you might not be strong enough to survive.

How I survived abuse, hurt and pain was through prayer, faith in God and never giving up.